OUI LOVE NUMBERS

An English/French Bilingual Counting Book

by Oui Love Books

ODÉON LIVRE
CHICAGO
2018

odeonlivre.com

Il y a **un** zèbre.

There is **one** zebra.

UN / ONE

Il y a **deux** éléphants.

There are **two** elephants.

2

DEUX / TWO

Il y a **trois** tomates.

There are **three** tomatoes.

3

TROIS / THREE

Il y a **quatre** poissons.

There are **four** fish.

QUATRE / FOUR

Il y a **cinq** pommes.

There are **five** apples.

5

CINQ / FIVE

Il y a **six** canards.

There are **six** ducks.

SIX / SIX

Il y a **sept** pastèques.

There are **seven** watermelons.

7

SEPT / SEVEN

Il y a **huit** lions.

There are **eight** lions.

8

HUIT / EIGHT

Il y a **neuf** carottes.

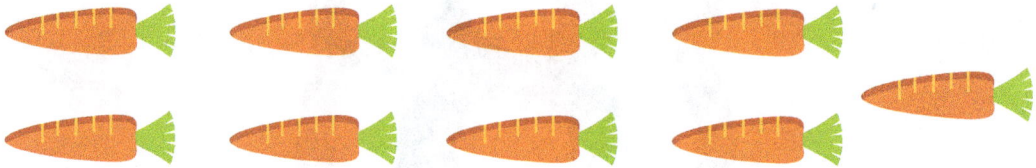

There are **nine** carrots.

9

NEUF / NINE

Il y a **dix** écureuils.

There are **ten** squirrels.

10

DIX / TEN

1 UN

2 DEUX

3 TROIS

4 QUATRE

5 CINQ

6 SIX

7 SEPT

8 HUIT

9 NEUF

10 DIX

1	un
2	deux
3	trois
4	quatre
5	cinq
6	six
7	sept
8	huit
9	neuf
10	dix

1

ONE

2

TWO

3

THREE

4

FOUR

5

FIVE

6

SIX

7

SEVEN

8

EIGHT

9

NINE

10

TEN

1	one
2	two
3	three
4	four
5	five
6	six
7	seven
8	eight
9	nine
10	ten

1	un	one
2	deux	two
3	trois	three
4	quatre	four
5	cinq	five
6	six	six
7	sept	seven
8	huit	eight
9	neuf	nine
10	dix	ten

1	I
2	II
3	III
4	IV
5	V
6	VI
7	VII
8	VIII
9	IX
10	X

www.ingramcontent.com/pod-product-compliance
Lightning Source LLC
Chambersburg PA
CBHW050639150426
42813CB00054B/1117